D0996690

Charles
DARWIN

Cath Senker

Wayland

an imprint of Hodder Children's Books

© 2001 White-Thomson Publishing Ltd

Produced for Hodder Wayland by
White-Thomson Publishing Ltd
2/3 St Andrew's Place
Lewes
BN7 1UP

Editor: Polly Goodman
Designer: Malcolm Walker
Picture Researcher: Shelley Noronha, Glass Onion Pictures
Cover and Title Page Illustrator: Richard Hook
Science Panel Illustrator: Derek Lee
Consultant: Dr Brian Bowers, Senior Research Fellow at the
Science Museum, London.

Published in Great Britain in 2001 by Hodder Wayland, an imprint
of Hodder Children's Books.

British Library Cataloguing in Publication Data
Senker, Cath
    Charles Darwin. - (Scientists Who Made History)
    1. Darwin, Charles, 1809–1882
    2. Biologists - Great Britain
    3. Evolution (Biology)
    I. Title
    576.8'2'092

ISBN 0 7502 3331 1

Printed and bound in Italy by G. Canale & C.S.p.A, Turin

Hodder Children's Books
A division of Hodder Headline Limited
338 Euston Road, London, NW1 3BH

Picture Acknowledgements: AKG 24, 30, 33; Bridgeman 10, 14b, 21,
22, 35t, 37; Bruce Coleman 4, 5, 14t, 16t&b, 32, 35b, 41b;
Cambridgeshire Collection, Cambridge Central Library 11b;
Darwin Archive, by permission of the Syndics of Cambridge
University Library 38; Mary Evans 6, 7, 9b, 13, 15, 17, 18, 26, 29,
31, 34, 36, 39t&b, 42; Fotomas Index 11t, 20t, 25; Hodder Wayland
Picture Library 8t&b, 19t&b, 20b, 28, 40; Oxford Scientific Films
27; Popperfoto 40, 41t; Chris Schwarz 43; Topham 41; University
College London 23 (Galton papers 9).

Contents

Mysterious Islands

IN THEIR OWN WORDS

'We landed upon black, dismal-looking heaps of broken lava, forming a shore fit for pandemonium [wild disorder]. Innumerable crabs and hideous iguanas started in every direction as we scrambled from rock to rock.'

ROBERT FITZROY, CAPTAIN OF THE H.M.S. BEAGLE, IN HIS MEMOIRS OF THE JOURNEY.

IT WAS 15 SEPTEMBER 1835 when the H.M.S. *Beagle* reached Chatham, one of the Galápagos islands. A young British naturalist by the name of Charles Darwin and the crew of the ship were nearing the end of a five-year voyage around the world.

At first sight, Chatham Island seemed an ugly, uninviting place. The crew looked upon vast heaps of black volcanic rock on the shore. Dozens of volcanoes rose 30 metres into the air. The ground was covered with black cinders. Darwin found them burning hot and painful to walk upon. The air was warm and sticky, and there was an unpleasant smell.

But if it was hell for humans, the island appeared to be a paradise for huge reptiles. Turtles glided around the bay.

BELOW: *A view of one of the Galápagos islands today, with a volcano in the background and a seal basking in the shallows. The black rocks are volcanic, made from the hardened lava from a volcano.*

Further inland, there were giant tortoises 4 metres in circumference, plodding around clumsily and munching on prickly pears. Vast numbers of marine iguanas – strange, seaweed-eating creatures – slept on the shoreline rocks.

The birds on the island were tame – they obviously had no predators. Darwin poked at a hawk with the barrel of his gun and it simply gazed at him. There was no sport to be had here. The crew shot eighteen giant tortoises and hauled them aboard to eat as fresh meat.

After five weeks of travelling around the Galápagos islands, the *Beagle*'s crew members were glad to leave this strange, uncomfortable place. As he dined on tortoise meat over the next few weeks, Darwin had little idea that these hostile islands would provide the key to his revolutionary theories of evolution.

BELOW: *An adult marine iguana with its young on its back. At the time Darwin visited the Galápagos islands, scientists believed that marine iguanas came from mainland South America. Later, Darwin realized that these animals were found only on the Galápagos and nowhere else.*

DARWIN'S WORLD

When Darwin was born, at the beginning of the nineteenth century, most people in Britain still lived in the countryside. They worked on farms or in small businesses. Most were also Christians, who went to church on Sundays and believed in God. The common view was that everyone had their place in life. The ruling class, led by the king, owned most of the land and held most of the power. Then there were many ranks, down through the middle classes, to the poorest, landless farmworkers. People believed that society was fixed by God and could not be changed. Scientists usually made their discoveries fit in with the Bible, too.

BELOW: *An illustration of the opening of the Stockton-to-Darlington railway, England, in 1825. The growth of the railways was an important part of Britain's Industrial Revolution. Goods could now be moved quickly and cheaply around the country by train.*

ABOVE: *Machinery being used in a stocking factory in Tewkesbury, England, in 1860. You can see lists of rules for the workers on the right-hand wall. By bringing together many workers in one place who used machinery, factories could produce larger amounts of goods than when people made them by hand.*

Yet Britain in the early 1800s was changing rapidly. The steam engine had been invented in the eighteenth century and factories, powered by steam, were being set up to make goods quickly and cheaply. This was the start of the Industrial Revolution.

Society was beginning to change, too. A growing middle class of people, who invested in the new industries, needed practical inventions. These would help them to develop new ways of making things. They wanted science based on experiments rather than religious beliefs. Working people were also starting to question the biblical view of the world.

IN THEIR OWN WORDS

'*That which hath been is that which will be. And that which has been done is that which will be done. So there is nothing new under the sun.*'

FROM THE BOOK OF ECCLESIASTES IN THE OLD TESTAMENT OF THE BIBLE, WHICH SUMS UP THE CHURCH OF ENGLAND'S VIEW OF THE WORLD.

Early Years

CHARLES ROBERT DARWIN was born on
12 February 1809, near Shrewsbury, England. His father,
Robert, was a doctor, and his mother, Susannah, was the
daughter of Josiah Wedgwood, who built up the famous
Wedgwood pottery industry. Charles was the fifth of six
children in this wealthy, middle-class family.

As a young boy, Charles loved to wander off on his own
around the grounds of the family's huge home, called The
Mount. His father loved plants, so there were exotic fruit
trees and rare shrubs to discover, and his mother kept fancy
pigeons. A mischievous child, one of Charles' earliest
memories was of trying to break the window in a room he
had been locked in as a punishment.

ABOVE: *A portrait of Charles'*
grandfather, Erasmus Darwin
(1731–1802). Erasmus had his
own early theories about
evolution, which he published in
a book called **Zoonomia**. *In the*
book, Erasmus described his
ideas about how the environment
affects living things.

LEFT: *A portrait of Charles'*
father, Robert Darwin. Robert
thought that Charles spent too
much time on his hobbies and
did not study hard enough.

LEFT: *A drawing of Charles aged about five years old, with his sister Catherine. Charles was interested in nature from an early age. Here he is shown with a plant that he has been growing.*

Charles loved to spend hours fishing by the river, using worms he'd collected himself for bait. Collecting things was Charles' greatest hobby. All sorts of things fascinated him, from shells, to birds' eggs and postal franks.

His mother died when Charles was eight, and from then on he was brought up by his father and three elder sisters. The atmosphere at home was tense. All lived in fear of their father, with his strict rules of behaviour.

In 1818, aged nine, Charles was sent to boarding school. There he was extremely bored by the lessons, which were in Latin and Greek, and he didn't do well in school. He enjoyed his hobbies far more than his school work. One year, Charles and his brother Erasmus took an interest in chemistry. They set up a laboratory in the garden shed and created lots of stinking gases. As a teenager, one of Charles' favourite pastimes was going hunting.

IN THEIR OWN WORDS

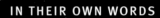

'[Charles would] invent deliberate falsehoods... for the pure pleasure of exciting attention and surprise.'

JOSIAH WEDGWOOD, DESCRIBING DARWIN AS A BOY.

BLOOD, GUTS AND BOTANY

In 1825, aged sixteen, Charles Darwin was packed off to
Edinburgh University in Scotland to study medicine. His
father had decided that Charles would follow in his own
footsteps and become a doctor. Charles went to Edinburgh
with his brother, Erasmus, who was also studying medicine.
The two young men thought that the city of Edinburgh was
beautiful, and they enjoyed the drinking and gambling of
student life.

But Charles absolutely hated medicine. He found the
lectures dull and he couldn't bear the horrors of surgery.
In the early nineteenth century, surgeons in dirty clothing
hacked off limbs with filthy saws, while the patients
screamed in agony. During a particularly bad operation on
a child, Charles walked out, vowing never again to enter an
operating theatre.

BELOW: *An eighteenth-century
illustration of a man having his
leg amputated while student
doctors watch from the right.
It was not until the 1840s that
patients were given anaesthetic
gases to breathe in order to dull
the pain.*

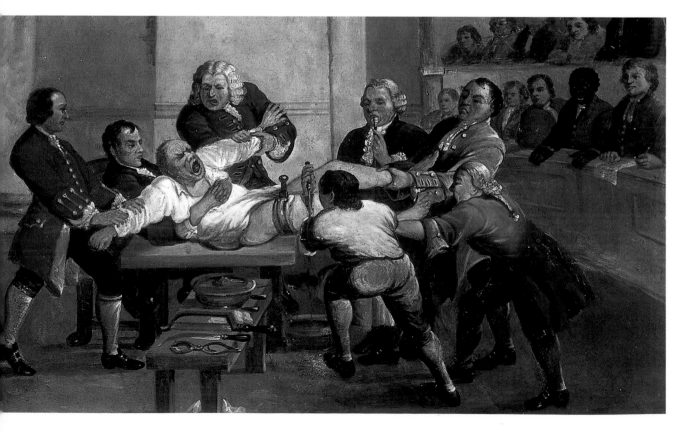

THE DIVINE DESIGNER

At the time Charles Darwin was studying at Cambridge, the most popular theory about how the natural world was formed was by the Reverend William Paley. He argued that things in nature were so perfectly designed for their role in life that they could not possibly have come into being by themselves. There had to have been a divine creator, which was God. This theory also fitted the Creation story in the Bible, which said that God created the world and everything in it in seven days. As a student, Darwin accepted Paley's argument, but he soon saw the problems with it.

Cambridge

In 1828, Charles moved to Cambridge University to study to become a clergyman in the Church of England. His father believed this would be a good job for an aimless son. It would provide a comfortable living, too. As a clergyman, Charles would have a fine country home with a few hectares of land, and could spend much of his time enjoying his favourite hobbies of collecting plants and animals, and hunting.

At Cambridge, Darwin became friendly with the geologist Adam Sedgwick and botanist John Henslow, and his interest in rocks, animals and plants grew. He joined the beetle craze, where wealthy young gentlemen travelled around the country looking for rare and unusual beetles to add to their collections. Yet Darwin studied hard enough to pass his exams at Cambridge, and in 1831 he was awarded a Bachelor of Arts degree.

BELOW: *An engraving showing the view from Darwin's rooms at Christ's College, Cambridge, where he studied for three years. Darwin loved going to John Henslow's botany lectures and was constantly asking him questions about plants.*

The Voyage of the *Beagle*

BELOW, MAIN MAP: *The Beagle's route. From England, the ship crossed the Atlantic and made several trips up and down the coasts of South America, before sailing west across the Pacific to New Zealand and Australia.*

INSET MAP: *Britain and the places where Darwin lived.*

THE TIME WAS RIPE for Darwin to become a clergyman and settle down. But he didn't feel ready yet. He had just read Alexander Humboldt's *Personal Narrative*, in which the writer described a fascinating voyage he made around South America from 1799 to 1804. Darwin decided that the discovery of lush, tropical forests and rugged volcanoes was just the thing for him.

In August 1831, Darwin was offered a position on the H.M.S. *Beagle*. The captain, Robert FitzRoy, was about to set sail for South America on a two-year mission to make maps for the Royal Navy. Darwin would be the ship's naturalist and companion to the captain. Darwin's father was horrified at this reckless plan and refused to pay for the trip. But his closest friend and brother-in-law Jos Wedgwood persuaded him to let his son go. Darwin was overjoyed.

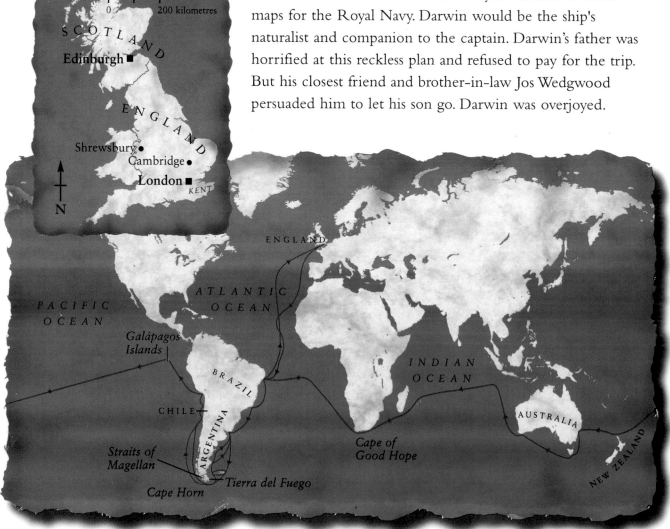

0   150 miles
0   200 kilometres

SCOTLAND
Edinburgh ■

ENGLAND
Shrewsbury ●
Cambridge ●
London ■
KENT

N

ENGLAND

ATLANTIC OCEAN

PACIFIC OCEAN

Galápagos Islands

BRAZIL

INDIAN OCEAN

CHILE

ARGENTINA

AUSTRALIA

Straits of Magellan

Cape of Good Hope

NEW ZEALAND

Cape Horn

Tierra del Fuego

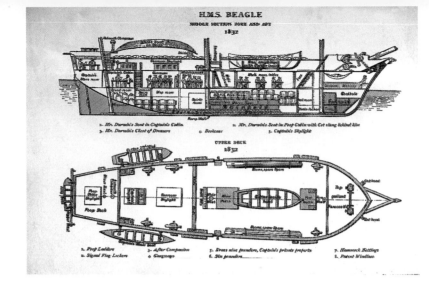

LEFT: *This drawing shows the layout of the Beagle. The ship was tiny — only 27 metres long and 7.3 metres wide. Darwin shared a cabin with one of the officers. He slept in a hammock above the chart table.*

Seasickness and specimens

In December, the H.M.S. *Beagle* set sail, and Darwin's misery began straight away. He was horribly seasick. For ten days he could keep no food down except dry biscuits and raisins. He was to suffer from seasickness throughout the voyage.

Darwin's spirits perked up when the *Beagle* arrived in South America. They landed at Bahia, in Salvador, and Darwin set foot in an amazing world. He was completely amazed by the thick vegetation, fantastic flowers and countless varieties of insects.

While on his travels, Darwin shipped back vast quantities of specimens, which provided great excitement for scientists back in Britain. Among the specimens were many fossils, including part of the fossil of an extinct giant sloth called Megatherium, and a giant llama-like creature. These finds set Darwin wondering why those animals had died out, and how they were related to similar animals that still existed.

FOSSILS

In Darwin's time, the accepted view of fossils came from the Creation story in the Bible. It was believed that all fossils were formed at the same time, after one great disaster such as Noah's flood, which wiped out most living things. But the evidence from the rocks showed that fossils from nearer the surface were more similar to animals and plants living in the present day than those from deeper layers. It seemed that the earlier animals and plants had gradually died out, to be replaced by others. But until Darwin's groundbreaking theory, no one knew exactly how this happened.

Fish fossil from layer nearer the surface.

Ammonite fossil from a deeper layer.

INCREDIBLE CHANGING WORLD

During the *Beagle* voyage, Darwin saw dramatic things that set his mind bubbling about how things change in the natural world. He puzzled over why animals and plants varied in different areas. For example, in Patagonia, there were two varieties of rhea (ostrich-like birds), living in different parts of the country. Why were there two varieties and why had they separated? The mysteries of the fossils added to the puzzle. Long-dead plants and animals were similar but not the same as those living in the present.

While on board, Darwin read Charles Lyell's *Principles of Geology*, which was published in 1830. Lyell wrote that all the processes of nature, such as coastal erosion, go on at the same rate, so they must have been going on for millions of years. Over an extremely long time, they shaped the Earth we see today.

ABOVE: *This bird is a greater rhea. Darwin saw two types of rhea in the Galápagos: greater and smaller. At first, Darwin wondered if one type of rhea had been born from the other, as a kind of 'freak', and had gone on to create a new species. He later realized that they had both evolved into different species.*

BELOW: *An engraving of the* **Beagle** *in the Straits of Magellan, which cut through the southern tip of South America. Local people from Tierra del Fuego are shown in three dug-out canoes around the ship.*

Later, in 1835, Darwin witnessed a terrible earthquake in Chile. Earthquakes are caused when huge pressures under the Earth build up over time, and then are suddenly released. Pondering over the earthquake, Darwin started thinking that if the landscape had been changing throughout history, then living things must also have changed.

People seemed to vary quite a lot as well. In December 1832, the *Beagle* landed at Tierra del Fuego, at the southernmost tip of South America. Captain FitzRoy wanted to return three Fuegians (people from Tierra del Fuego), who had been living in England. Darwin was shocked to see the local Fuegians. They wore few clothes, painted their faces and slept on the wet ground. How were they related to an educated Englishman like himself?

IN THEIR OWN WORDS

'When we were on the shore, the party looked rather alarmed, but continued talking and making gestures with great rapidity. It was without exception the most curious and interesting spectacle I had ever beheld. I could not have believed how wide was the difference between savage and civilized man. It is greater than that between a wild and domesticated animal, in as much as in man there is a greater power of improvement.'

DARWIN IN 1832, FROM THE DIARY HE WROTE ON HIS VOYAGE.

RIGHT: *An engraving made in about 1860 showing indigenous people from Tierra del Fuego.*

Galápagos islands

In September 1835, the *Beagle* left the west coast of South America and set off across the Pacific Ocean. About 1,000 kilometres from the mainland of Lima, Peru, the ship reached a group of around thirteen small, rocky volcanic islands – the Galápagos islands. This was a short, five-week stop near the end of a long and exhausting voyage. But it was to have great significance for Darwin's theory of evolution.

The huge reptiles and strange birds of the Galápagos were like no others that Darwin had ever come across. Yet they seemed to have some things in common with species on the South American mainland. What was the relationship between them?

More curious was the fact that each island had its very own kinds of plants and animals, slightly different from the ones found on the other islands. Each had its own varieties of strange and beautiful orchids, and different kinds of finches. There were giant tortoises, large enough for the

ABOVE: *A Galápagos giant tortoise. Darwin later worked out that the prisoners on the Galápagos had been right – each island had its own type of tortoise. Each type was adapted to living on its own particular island.*

BELOW: *Bartholomew Island in the Galápagos. Today, the Galápagos islands are protected as a nature reserve. Yet their unique plants and animals are under threat from the effects of tourism and pollution, such as a spill from an oil tanker in January 2001.*

THE GALÁPAGOS FINCHES

The Galápagos finches provided a key to Darwin's theory of evolution. Found nowhere else in the world, each species of finch had a slightly different beak, which was suited to a particular kind of food.

The Galápagos islands formed relatively recently in the history of the Earth, just a few million years ago. A few finches probably landed there from the mainland of South America, perhaps blown to the islands in a storm. Food was plentiful. The original species of finch gradually evolved into many different species, each suited to eating a different kind of food. This meant that the birds did not compete with each other. The finches showed how, over time, species change to suit their environment.

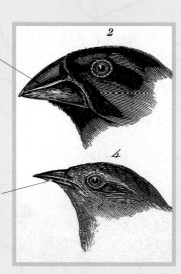

Large ground finch has a huge beak for cracking tough seeds.

Small ground finch has a small, strong beak for cracking small, hard seeds.

Medium ground finch has a smaller beak, for cracking smaller seeds.

Warbler finch has a long, slim beak for probing into cracks in trees and catching insects.

ship's crew to ride like horses. A group of exiled prisoners from Ecuador, who were living on one of the islands, claimed they could tell which island a tortoise came from by the shape of its shell.

Back on board the *Beagle*, Darwin didn't bother labelling which islands all his different finch specimens came from. It was only when he got back to England that he realized the differences between the Galápagos animals were incredibly important.

ABOVE: *Illustrations of some of the different kinds of finches discovered by Darwin. This example of evolution has become so famous that the birds are often known as 'Darwin's finches'.*

COLONIZERS OR CIVILIZERS?

'[They were] clean, tidy and healthy in appearance, like that of dairy maids in England...I never saw a nicer or more merry group, and to think that this was in the centre of the land of cannibalism, murder and all atrocious crimes!'

DARWIN, WRITING IN HIS DIARY ABOUT THE
MAORI SERVANT GIRLS IN NEW ZEALAND.

THE NEXT LEG of the *Beagle's* journey took the crew to Tahiti, New Zealand and Australia. To Darwin, Tahiti was a tropical paradise of bananas, coconuts and breadfruit trees. Even delicious guavas grew everywhere, like weeds. Tahiti was an island where missionaries were established. European Christians went there to convert the local people to Christianity and guide them towards adopting a European lifestyle.

Darwin was impressed. He saw the 'laughing merry faces' of the Tahitians, their neat clothes and the friendly welcome they gave visitors. To his understanding, typical of a wealthy Victorian, this meant the Tahitians were climbing the scale of civilization, which had Europeans at the top. More questions came to mind. Did people develop over time, and if so, were earlier humans very different? This idea conflicted with the biblical view that people were a fixed type, created by God.

RIGHT: *An illustration from about 1850 of Hororwowa (left), a Maori chief in New Zealand who was converted to Christianity. Darwin firmly believed that it was right to make other peoples become Christians and adopt a European lifestyle. He felt it made them better, more civilized people.*

ABOVE: *This painting shows the arrival of the first governor of New South Wales in Sydney, Australia, on 26 January 1788. The governor is about to propose a toast to King George III of England, as the Union Jack flag is raised to show that the land is claimed by Britain.*

New Zealand and Australia

The next stop was New Zealand, where the local Maoris had suffered unspeakable horrors. Almost entirely wiped out by the Europeans taking over the country at the time, the few who remained were being forced to become Christians. In Australia, too, where the *Beagle* landed in January 1836, the indigenous Aborigines were being killed, or were dying from European diseases and lack of food. Darwin wondered whether the human world was just like the animal world, where the strong always seemed to destroy the weak. If God had created all the people in the world at the same time, as told in the Bible's Creation story, why did he make them all so different?

ABOVE: *A photograph of an Australian aborigine in front of his temporary shelter in the late nineteenth century.*

Home at Last

AFTER LEAVING AUSTRALIA in March 1836, Darwin was keen to get home. Seven months later, on the stormy night of 2 October 1836, the *Beagle* arrived in Falmouth, England. After his spectacular travels, Darwin faced the huge task of sorting out his finds, which included 1,529 species bottled in spirits and 3,907 labelled specimens. Just as importantly, he needed to think about all the questions that were whirring around inside his head. The real work was about to begin.

Using his 770-page diary and other journals, Darwin started work on a book about the events of the *Beagle* voyage, which he called the *Journal of Researches*. He also began writing other books on zoology and coral reefs.

Meanwhile he decided it was time to find a wife. His first cousin, Emma Wedgwood, had caught his eye. Both families approved of the match, and the couple married in 1838. Since Darwin's personal and working life were never far apart, he started writing in his notebooks about mating in animals. In 1839, Darwin published his *Journal of Researches*, which he'd been working on for the past three years.

ABOVE: *A case of beetles from Darwin's collection. Darwin had always been a careful collector. Keeping samples of plants and animals and writing notes about them were vital to his success as a scientist.*

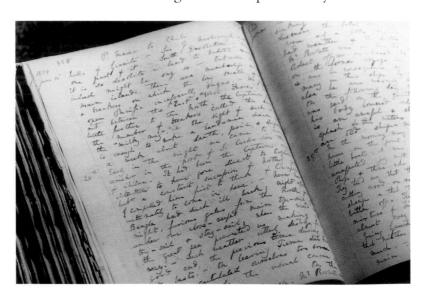

RIGHT: *Pages of Darwin's diary that he wrote while on the* Beagle's *voyage. Throughout his life, Darwin kept a personal diary as well as writing notes on his research.*

ABOVE: *A portrait of Emma Darwin, shortly after her marriage to Charles.*

The journal's publication was hugely successful. The same year, in 1839, Charles and Emma bought a house in Upper Gower Street, London. Their first child, William, was born in December 1839. As soon as Willy arrived, Darwin started taking notes on the baby's first signs of anger, fear and pleasure. He was thinking about the origins of humans, and he wanted to compare his baby's expressions with the behaviour of Jenny Orang, an orang-utan in London Zoo.

After a few years, Darwin decided that London, with all its traffic and chaos, was no place to bring up a family. On 17 September 1842, he collected their valuables and slammed the door on 12 Upper Gower Street for the last time. The Darwins were moving to the country.

IN THEIR OWN WORDS

<u>Marry</u>

1. Children

2. Constant companion... object to be beloved and played with – better than a dog anyhow

3. Home, and someone to take care of house

4. ...it is intolerable to think of spending one's whole life... working, working, and nothing after all. Only picture to yourself a nice, soft wife on a sofa with a good fire, and books and music...

<u>Not Marry</u>

1. Freedom to go where one liked

2. Not forced to visit relatives... [or] to have the expense and anxiety of children

3. Loss of time... fatness and idleness

4. If many children, forced to gain one's bread [earn money] – (but then it is very bad for one's health to work too much)

A SHORTENED LIST OF THE PROS AND CONS THAT DARWIN WROTE WHEN CONSIDERING GETTING MARRIED.

LIFE IN THE COUNTRY

The Darwins' new home was Down House in Kent, the kind of country house Darwin had dreamt of when he was thinking of becoming a clergyman. Deep in the countryside, 12 kilometres from the nearest railway station, it was ideal for a gentleman naturalist. In a letter to an old servant, Covington, he noted, 'This will be my direction [address] for the rest of my life.'

Over the following years, the Darwin family grew rapidly. Ten children were born to Charles and Emma, but three died in childhood. In mid-nineteenth-century England, even the wealthy were not spared the tragedy of frequent childhood deaths.

BELOW: *Down House, the Darwins' home in Kent, as it is today. Darwin was a very private man. When the family moved into their new home, he had a 2-metre wall built around the property so that no one could look in.*

LEFT: *A photograph of Darwin with his eldest son, William, in 1842. This is the only known photograph of Darwin with a member of his family. Darwin was devoted to his children and worried constantly about their health and education. Since he worked from home, he was able to spend time playing with them. As they grew older, some of his children helped him out with his experiments.*

Emma was a devoted wife to Darwin, who demanded her constant attention. He couldn't bear for her to be away from him. Even when Emma's mother died in 1846, and she had to go away for a short while over the summer, Darwin fretted endlessly and complained of loneliness.

Darwin was a man who liked a peaceful life with a fixed routine. He didn't like visiting people and there were few guests at Down House. Darwin described his days there as being as alike 'as two peas'. He would get up at 7 am and work until 10 am, when he and Emma would have breakfast and relax. Then he worked until lunch at 2 pm. After lunch, he might go into town, returning for dinner and a quiet evening reading and listening to music. Most of Darwin's days were spent in this way.

IN THEIR OWN WORDS

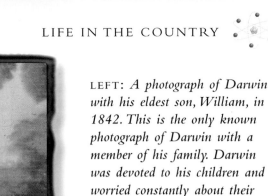

'I am an ungracious old dog to howl, for I have been... thinking what a fortunate man I am, so well-off in worldly circumstances, with such dear little children and... more than all with such a wife.'

DARWIN COUNTING HIS BLESSINGS DURING EMMA'S ABSENCE, IN THE SUMMER OF 1846.

A SICK MAN

Darwin had been a fit man during the *Beagle* voyage, tramping across the grassy South American plains and climbing mountains with ease. Once he returned to England, however, he became ill.

The illnesses Darwin suffered from were many and varied. They ranged from skin problems to headaches, stomach pains and broken sleep. Often, he could only work a few hours a day. We know this from Darwin's careful records of the number of working days he lost due to illness. He couldn't take part fully in scientific debates because he never appeared in public. Yet he exchanged letters with many well-known scientists.

IN THEIR OWN WORDS

'When relations unite... there is a decrease in general vigour.'

DARWIN, IN *THE ORIGIN OF SPECIES*, ABOUT THE DANGERS OF INBREEDING WITHIN FAMILIES SUCH AS HIS OWN.

RIGHT: *A watercolour portrait of Darwin in 1840, when he was thirty-one years old. Darwin's illnesses made him miserable. In 1840, he moaned to Charles Lyell that he hadn't been able to work for nine whole weeks. His achievements in science are even more amazing when you consider how ill he was for much of the time.*

There are several theories about Darwin's illnesses. Did he catch a tropical disease while travelling around the world? Did he have lots of allergies, or perhaps ME – an illness that makes people very tired and depressed? Or was his ill-health brought on by stress?

Darwin was terrified that he had passed on his ill-health to his children, who were often ill, too. Various cures were attempted with mixed results.

In the late 1840s, when Darwin was about forty years old, he was frail and barely able to walk. He tried a cure called hydropathy, which involved a special diet, taking homeopathic remedies and being scrubbed with cold water every day. The cure seemed to work at first, but the effects did not last, and Darwin was dogged by ill-health for the rest of his life.

BELOW: *A photograph of Darwin's microscope, which was one of his most important pieces of equipment. Another was his gun, which he used to shoot many of his animal specimens.*

A Theory Evolves

IN THEIR OWN WORDS

'I think I have found out (here's presumption!) the simple way by which species become exquisitely adapted to various ends.'

Darwin, writing to his friend, the botanist Joseph Dalton Hooker, in late 1843.

AT THIS TIME in Britain, most people believed in the biblical story of Creation. One churchman, Archbishop Usher, actually worked out from the Bible when the world was created, and came up with the date 4004 BC. It was thought that human beings were special, made by God to be better than animals. But some people already had their doubts about the biblical version of events.

Geologists such as Charles Lyell had already shown that the Earth was older than the Bible said. Fossils showed that some animals and plants had lived in the past but had died out. The fact that there were living animals and plants that were similar to species that had died out led some scientists to suggest that living things evolved, or changed over time.

BELOW: *Darwin's study in Down House, cluttered with books and papers. Darwin kept notebooks on different subjects, including his diary and secret notebooks where he wrote down his ideas about evolution long before making them public.*

DARWIN'S THEORY OF NATURAL SELECTION

Darwin's theory of evolution was that plants and animals change over time through a process of natural selection. It works like this:

1. Parents have young that are similar, but slightly different to themselves.

2. More young are born than can survive. The young with features that are better suited to their environment survive and breed.

3. The plants and animals that survive, breed and pass on the useful features to their own young.

4. Over time, these tiny variations in features mean that species change.

5. Species that are best adapted to their environment do well. The ones that are poorly adapted die out.

Several scientists had come up with theories of evolution. Around 1800, French naturalist Jean-Baptiste Lamarck (1744–1829) developed the idea that animals could change depending on the environment they lived in. For example, giraffes needed to feed from high trees, so they grew longer necks. Then their babies were born with longer necks.

Since 1837, Darwin had secretly been building his own theory of evolution. He agreed with Lamarck that plants and animals had evolved. But he did not believe that they changed within their own lifetime and passed on the changes to their offspring. Darwin was the first to work out how evolution really happened.

RIGHT: *A giraffe reaching for leaves in Kenya. We now know that the giraffe's long neck is set in its genes, and cannot change during the lifetime of one animal.*

DANGEROUS IDEAS

The more Darwin researched the evolution of the natural world, the more evidence he found that conflicted with the Creation story in the Bible. And if the Creation story was wrong, did that mean that other parts of the Bible, the basis of Christian beliefs, might be wrong too? Even though Darwin had developed his theory by 1842, he did not dare publish his ideas at first. He was terrified of the possible revolutionary effect it would have on English society. His social class, including all his good friends, was linked to the Church. Everyone would be horrified by a theory of Creation without God.

In the late 1830s and 1840s, a radical organization called the Chartists was making protests in Britain. The Chartists hated the common view that everyone had their place in life, decided by God. They wanted broad political changes, such as giving the vote to all men over the age of twenty-one, not just to those who owned property. The fear of Chartist demonstrators rioting through the streets had been one of the reasons the Darwin family left London. Darwin worried that his theory of evolution would encourage

BELOW: *Dancing at a high society party in London, in the nineteenth century. Many wealthy people liked the idea that everyone had a fixed place in life, decided by God. Yet Darwin's theory showed that human beings had developed just like plants and other animals. No special power made them different from the rest of the natural world.*

A portrait of Joseph Dalton Hooker (1817–1911). At first, Hooker did not accept Darwin's ideas on evolution, but he was prepared to discuss them and to test them out through his own research. Over time however, he became convinced that species could evolve into others, as Darwin suggested. Later, after Darwin published his theory of evolution, Hooker was one of his keenest supporters.

radicals like the Chartists by helping them to argue that if the world was always changing, society could change, too.

Yet Darwin could not keep quiet for ever. In 1844, he wrote an essay containing his main ideas about evolution and sent it to his good friend, the botanist Joseph Dalton Hooker, to read. As Darwin was quite ill at the time, he instructed his wife to publish the essay if he died. He realized that his theory would have to come out one day, even if it meant turning his comfortable world upside-down.

IN THEIR OWN WORDS

'I am almost convinced (quite contrary to the opinion I started with) that species are not (it is like confessing a murder) immutable [unchanging].'

DARWIN IN 1844, WRITING TO JOSEPH HOOKER ABOUT HIS THEORY OF EVOLUTION AND COMPARING TALKING ABOUT IT TO CONFESSING A MURDER.

ABOVE: *Revolutionaries tear down the palace of King Louis Philippe of France, in the February 1848 uprising in Paris. The king lost his throne, and the new French government allowed the people to vote for the first time. Revolutions quickly spread to the Austrian and German empires. It is not surprising that the wealthy classes in nearby England were worried by these events.*

TESTING TIMES

Darwin realized that he needed solid evidence to persuade the world that evolution was a serious theory, and not a mad scheme to uproot the Church. So he worked incredibly hard in the late 1840s and '50s to find evidence for his ideas.

In 1846, Darwin began a long, difficult and dull study of barnacles, which lasted for eight years. He used his findings to show how natural selection worked in practice. Darwin spent so much time with these little creatures that his children began to think it was normal for everyone's father to study barnacles.

The year of 1848 was one of revolutions in Europe and huge Chartist demonstrations in England. The European revolutions were democratic movements, mostly led by the middle classes, which wanted to have a say in government. The working classes joined them, sick of a life of poverty, ruled by kings and queens living in extreme wealth. Shortly after an uprising in Paris in February, the Chartists planned a protest of 150,000 people in London. Panic spread among the wealthy classes.

By the end of the year, all the uprisings had been put down. Yet Darwin's worries about the radical theory he was nursing kept his stress levels high. To add to the pressure Darwin faced, in 1850, his much-loved eldest daughter Annie became ill, and she died in 1851. Darwin was devastated. Her death put an end to his already shaken faith in Christianity and he could no longer believe in a just world.

BELOW: *The Chartist demonstration on Kennington Common, London, in April 1848. The Chartists held demonstrations to try and make the government listen to their demands.*

IN THEIR OWN WORDS

'She hardly ever required to be found fault with, and was never punished in any way whatever… every expression in her countenance [face] beamed with affection and kindness, and all her habits were influenced by her loving disposition [nature]… Oh that she could now know how deeply, how tenderly we do still and shall ever love her dear joyous face. Blessings on her.'

DARWIN, WRITING ABOUT HIS DAUGHTER ANNIE IN 1851, A WEEK AFTER SHE DIED.

COLLECTING AND SELECTING

In 1854, after putting away the barnacles, Darwin set up more experiments to test out his theory of natural selection. Friends, other scientists and his own children helped out. Darwin decided to investigate domestic animals. Down House stank of duck meat as Darwin boiled up the animals' bodies to compare the skeletons of wild ducks with those of domestic ones.

No other gentleman scientist had done this kind of research since it was seen as rather undignified to get one's hands dirty messing about with farm animals. But Darwin realized that when people bred animals, their work might be similar to the process of evolution in nature.

He spent time in gin palaces and beer halls talking to working-class pigeon breeders, who could spot the tiniest variation in the size of a pigeon's tail. For example, by breeding pigeons with the broadest tail feathers, over time the breeders had produced the fantail pigeon. They had created so many differences within domestic pigeons that if the pigeons were found in the wild, they would be classed as completely different species.

RIGHT: *A hen-white exhibition fantail pigeon. Working-class men in Darwin's time took pride in raising prize pigeons as a hobby. Darwin paid many of them to help him out with his research, and they welcomed his interest in their hobby. In the clubs of Borough, in south London, he became known as the 'Squire'.*

LEFT: *A photograph of Darwin in 1863, taken from the second edition of* The Origin of Species. *Darwin encouraged young scientists such as Hooker and Huxley, who began to get important jobs in science in the 1850s. They helped to spread new scientific ideas that did not fit in with the biblical view of the world.*

Here was more evidence for Darwin's theory of natural selection. Breeders used artificial selection. They mated animals according to particular features they wanted passed on to their young. It seemed they were simply speeding up what happened in nature anyway.

By the mid–1850s, Darwin had a few close friends who were starting to accept his views on evolution. As well as Joseph Hooker, young scientists Thomas Huxley and Alfred Russel Wallace shared some of his ideas. By 1856, Darwin felt brave enough to start writing a book for publication.

IN THEIR OWN WORDS

'I cannot swallow Man [being that] distinct from a Chimpanzee... I wonder what a Chimpanzee would say to this?'

DARWIN IN 1857, RESPONDING TO CHRISTIAN SCIENTIST RICHARD OWEN'S CLAIM THAT HUMANS WERE IN A SEPARATE CLASS FROM ANIMALS.

The Secret's Out!

IN 1858, DARWIN was still working on his huge book on evolution when, all of a sudden, the bottom dropped out of his world. On 18 June, he received a letter from fellow scientist Alfred Russel Wallace. Inside, Wallace described how evolution occurred, in words close to Darwin's own.

Darwin was friends with Wallace and had shared ideas with him. But if Wallace's theory came out first, Darwin's work would not seem original and twenty years of work would be wasted. Success would go to the man who published first: Wallace. Yet Wallace had sent him the work in trust and Darwin could not betray him.

There was no choice. They would have to publish together – and fast. On 30 June, Darwin and Wallace's joint paper on the theory of evolution was presented at a meeting of the Linnean Society, a scientific society in London. Surprisingly, the paper was greeted with silence and lack of interest. The President of the Linnean Society walked out of the meeting, disappointed, as he later put it, that the year had not been marked by any 'striking discoveries'. Darwin was not at

RIGHT: *A photograph of the British naturalist Alfred Russel Wallace (1823–1913). While in the Spice Islands of Indonesia, Wallace developed his theory of evolution, which was similar to that of Darwin. The two naturalists continued to debate the theory of evolution and remained friends for the rest of their lives.*

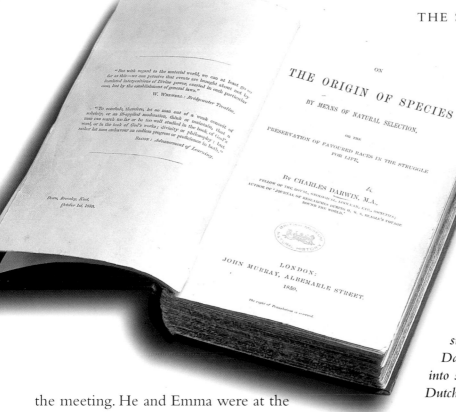

LEFT: The first edition of The Origin of Species, *published in 1859, which is now kept in the Natural History Museum, London. By 1871, six editions had been published. Darwin's book was translated into several languages, including Dutch, French, Italian and German.*

the meeting. He and Emma were at the funeral of their baby son, Charles, who had just died of scarlet fever.

The Origin of Species

Despite the lack of interest from the Linnean Society, Darwin continued work on his book and in 1859, *On The Origin of Species by Means of Natural Selection* was finally published. It described how the process of natural selection made species evolve. All species were created and changed by nature. God was not involved. Darwin awaited the reaction to his theory with bated breath, fearing he would be cast out of polite society for ever.

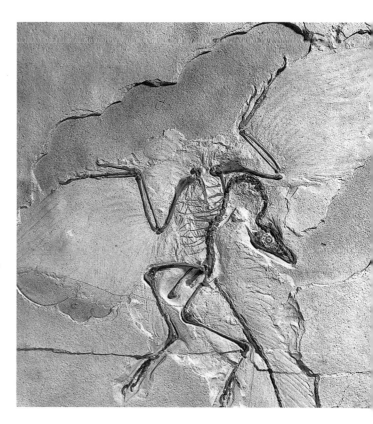

RIGHT: *The fossil of an archaeopteryx, discovered in Germany in 1861. This creature had a reptile's bones and tail – and feathers. It showed that birds had reptile ancestors, and helped to prove that living things evolved from one form into another.*

'MOST DANGEROUS MAN IN ENGLAND'

The publisher of *The Origin of Species*, John Murray, was so worried about the fuss that the book would cause that he only printed 1,250 copies. They sold out almost straight away as a fierce debate began throughout society.

Christians were outraged. Charles Darwin was denying that God had created the natural world and claimed that the biblical Creation story was untrue! Darwin knew that enemies like Richard Owen would hate his views, but others such as Adam Sedgwick, his Cambridge professor friend, also turned against him. One newspaper review labelled Darwin 'the most dangerous man in England'.

Yet some people were full of praise. Darwin's scientist friends Huxley, Hooker and Lyell formed a close circle of supporters. The pro-Darwin and the anti-Darwin camps now battled over evolution theory.

RIGHT: *A cartoon published in 1874 showing Darwin holding a mirror in front of an ape, to show how alike they are. After the publication of* **The Origin of Species,** *many popular newspapers wrote that Darwin was suggesting that people had evolved from living apes, such as gorillas. They were wrong.*

LEFT: *A drawing of the British naturalist Thomas Henry Huxley (1825–95) holding a skull in his hand. Huxley fought hard to establish himself as a scientist and became an enthusiastic supporter of Darwin's theory of evolution. He fiercely believed that religion should be kept out of science. Huxley believed that human beings evolved directly from apes, which we now know is not true.*

In 1860, there was a famous showdown during a scientific debate in Oxford. The big debate had Bishop Samuel Wilberforce, nicknamed 'Soapy Sam', defending God's role in the Creation of life. He was determined to 'smash Darwin'. On the other side were Darwin's supporters, Hooker and Huxley, fired up with determination to win the argument for natural selection. In a meeting crammed with about a thousand people, Darwin's supporters won the debate hands down.

The truth was that by 1860, the argument about evolution had been going on for a long time. Many people no longer believed the exact words of the Bible that said that God had created the world. They were looking for real, scientific answers to the mysteries of life, and were ready to accept Darwin's ideas.

A HERO AT LAST

Within a short time, most scientists came to accept Darwin's evolution theory. Thomas Huxley worked hard to spread Darwin's ideas in society. A natural teacher, he lectured to hundreds of working people on the origins of humans. The working classes welcomed proof that their low station in life was not fixed by God.

Darwin was also popular abroad. He received various awards from countries including France, Germany and Russia. The Germans were particularly keen on Darwin, and *The Origin of Species* sold well there.

Apart from his constant illness, Darwin's life became more settled. The daily routine at Down House went on as ever and the children were growing up. All Darwin's sons went on to have excellent careers and his daughter Henrietta helped him with some of his work.

The ageing scientist continued to write books throughout the 1860s and '70s. In 1871, eleven years after the publication of *The Origin of Species*, another book on evolution, *The Descent of Man,* was published. Here, Darwin made it clear that humans had evolved like other animals.

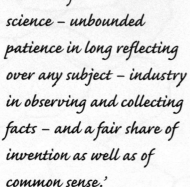

'...the most important [qualities] have been – the love of science – unbounded patience in long reflecting over any subject – industry in observing and collecting facts – and a fair share of invention as well as of common sense.'

DARWIN, WRITING IN HIS AUTOBIOGRAPHY IN 1876, DESCRIBING THE QUALITIES THAT MADE HIM A SUCCESSFUL SCIENTIST.

RIGHT: *The Darwin family at home at Down House, Kent, in 1863. From left to right: Leonard, Henrietta, Horace, Emma, Elizabeth, Francis and a visitor, with the family's dog lying in front. Henrietta Darwin helped her father to write* The Descent of Man *and was later the editor of* Emma Darwin: A Century of Family Letters, *which was first published in 1904.*

ABOVE: *A photo of Emma Darwin in later years. She continued to care for Charles right to the end, and accepted his death calmly.*

According to Darwin's theory of natural selection, the features of a living thing, such as its size, shape and colour, evolve to increase its chances of survival. But certain features, such as the peacock's colourful tail feathers, seem to reduce its chances by attracting predators. Darwin said that such features were an important part of sexual selection. The peacock's tail feathers help to attract female peahens so it can breed. Breeding successfully is part of survival.

The idea no longer came as a shock to his readers. He also wrote a fascinating book describing facial and bodily expressions in animals and people. Several books on plants and one on worms followed as a result of Darwin's experiments in his garden.

In 1881, Darwin fell ill and in April 1882, at the age of seventy-three, he died a painful death in Emma's loving arms. By this time, he had become an honoured figure in British society, and was buried in Westminster Abbey. But Darwin hadn't cared for honours. It was more important to him that his theories survived him.

ABOVE: *A photo of Darwin in later years. He continued working right up until his death in 1882.*

The Legacy of Darwin

ABOVE: *A laboratory worker in Israel, in June 2000, carrying out genetic research. By 2000, a rough map of all the genes that make up a human being had been completed.*

DARWIN'S THEORY OF EVOLUTION was a wonderful gift to science. It helped scientists to group animals and plants according to their common ancestor. They could now examine living things by looking at what each feature was for, and how it helped the plant or animal to survive and breed.

Fossils were no longer a mystery. They were the remains of dead plants and animals. Most had died out, while others had evolved into new species. Scientists could trace the pattern of evolution by looking at how fossils changed over time.

One thing that puzzled Darwin was how features are passed on from parent to offspring. While Darwin was working on *The Origin of Species*, a monk named Gregor Mendel was experimenting with peas in what is now Brno, in the Czech Republic. He worked out how features are passed on from one generation to the next, through what we now call genes. It wasn't until around 1900 that the importance of his work was recognized.

MENDEL'S DISCOVERIES

Mendel studied how features in peas were passed on from generation to generation. One of the features he tested was colour.

1. Mendel crossed plants that produced yellow peas with plants that produced green peas.

2. All the plants in the next generation produced yellow peas. The green peas seemed to have disappeared.

3. The yellow peas were planted and produced the next generation.

4. Of the 'grandchildren' of the original pea plants, three-quarters produced yellow peas, and one-quarter produced green peas.

Mendel had discovered that the colour of peas is decided by two pieces of information, passed on from the two parents. There is a 'factor' for green and a 'factor' for yellow. The yellow factor is dominant, so if the yellow factor is there at all, the plant will make yellow peas. If only the green factor is there, it will make green peas.

IN THEIR OWN WORDS

'No working biologist can read and understand Darwin's work without realizing the overwhelming importance it has had for the development of biological thought.'

JONATHAN HOWARD, FELLOW OF THE ROYAL SOCIETY, 1982.

LEFT: *In 1996, scientists produced a clone (exact copy) of a sheep, which had the same genes as its mother. They named the sheep Dolly. She became the world's first clone of a mammal.*

The study of how features are passed on became the science of genetics, which remains one of the hottest topics in science today. Since the 1980s, it has been discovered that the genetic material of humans differs by only 1 or 2 per cent from the genetic material of gorillas and chimpanzees. We are 99 per cent ape and only one per cent purely human. This evidence would have delighted Darwin, who realized that apes were our close relatives.

BELOW: *A female chimpanzee teaching her young what to eat. Darwin noticed that in many ways, young chimpanzees behave like human children.*

IN THEIR OWN WORDS

'The growth of large business is merely the survival of the fittest. It is merely the working out of a law of nature.'

US BUSINESSMAN, JOHN D. ROCKEFELLER (1839–1937), EXPLAINING HIS SUCCESS USING THE THEORY OF SOCIAL DARWINISM.

DARWINISM IN QUESTION

Many people, however, have never accepted Darwin's theory of evolution. Some Christians believe that every word of the Bible is true. According to their beliefs, the world is only a few thousand years old, as it says in the Bible. The fossils were placed on Earth by God. We are not related to apes because humans are special and did not come from animal origins. To these believers, evolution theory is simply a theory that has not been proved.

Social Darwinism

Darwin did not apply his theory of evolution to human society. But later thinkers took up his ideas and used them to try to explain why people in society are not equal. In the mid-1860s, Herbert Spencer, a fellow scientist of Darwin's, made up the phrase 'survival of the fittest'. The phrase has since been used to suggest that human society is a battle for the 'survival of the fittest'. This theory is called Social Darwinism.

According to Social Darwinism, people compete with one another to survive, and the 'fittest' people become richer and own more property. The theory suggests that poverty proves a person or group's weakness.

Many people do not agree with the theory of Social Darwinism. They believe that it does not consider many other

LEFT: *Herbert Spencer (1820–1903) in about 1890. Spencer agreed with Darwin's theory of evolution. He also believed that it could explain how human society evolved over time, from simple ways of life to complex industrial societies.*

LEFT: *Shoppers in Paris ignore a homeless man who is sitting on a hot-air vent to keep warm. According to the theory of Social Darwinism, poverty is a result of natural selection, so it is part of nature. Many people disagree with this theory.*

influences on wealth and poverty, such as the family into which you are born, and events in history.

Despite the debate over Social Darwinism, few people would disagree that Darwin's groundbreaking theory of evolution was an important contribution to modern science. Darwin would have been happy to know that his discoveries made it possible for us to understand ourselves better than ever before.

IN THEIR OWN WORDS

'Our ancestor was an animal which breathed water, had a swim bladder, a great swimming tail, an imperfect skull, and undoubtedly was a hermaphrodite [both male and female]!'

DARWIN TO CHARLES LYELL ABOUT THE ANIMAL
ORIGINS OF HUMANS, IN 1861.

Timeline

1798

Thomas Malthus writes an essay about how food supply cannot keep up with the growth of population. Darwin later uses these ideas when thinking about natural selection.

1801

Jean-Baptiste Lamarck publishes his early ideas on evolution. He says that animals change to adapt to their environment and pass on the changes to their offspring.

1809

12 FEBRUARY: Charles Darwin is born.

1815

18 JUNE: The Duke of Wellington defeats Napoleon at the Battle of Waterloo.

1817

15 JULY: Susannah Darwin, Charles' mother, dies.

1818

SEPTEMBER: Darwin is sent to boarding school.

1822

Rapid growth of cloth-producing factories in north-west England and lowland Scotland.

1824

Trade unions are allowed in England.

1825

The first steam railway service begins.

OCTOBER: Darwin goes to Edinburgh University.

1828

JANUARY: Darwin moves to Cambridge University.

1830

The first volume of Charles Lyell's *Principles of Geology* is published.

1831

DECEMBER: The H.M.S. *Beagle* sets sail on its voyage around the world.

1832

The Reform Act gives middle-class men over the age of twenty-one the right to vote in Britain.
DECEMBER: The *Beagle* lands at Tierra del Fuego, South America.

1835

FEBRUARY: Darwin sees an earthquake in Chile.
SEPTEMBER–DECEMBER: The *Beagle* visits the Galápagos islands, Tahiti and New Zealand.

1836

JANUARY: The *Beagle* lands in Australia.

2 OCTOBER: The *Beagle* arrives in Falmouth, England.

1837

Victoria is crowned Queen of the United Kingdom of Great Britain and Ireland.
Growth of railway building in Britain.
Darwin begins working on his theory of evolution.

1838

The Chartist movement demands the vote for workers.

1839

29 JANUARY: Charles Darwin and Emma Wedgwood are married.
Darwin's *Journal of Researches*, about the *Beagle* voyage, is published.
DECEMBER: The Darwins' first child, William, is born.

1842

SEPTEMBER: The Darwins move to Down House in Kent.

1844

Darwin writes an essay containing his theory of evolution, and sends it to Joseph Hooker.

1846

Darwin begins an eight-year study of barnacles.
The potato famine hits Ireland and also affects England and Wales. The farmers on Darwin's land are affected.
The British Government ends the Corn Laws to reduce the tax on bread.

1848

Revolutions sweep across Europe. Last big Chartist demonstrations in England. The Chartist movement collapses.

1851

APRIL: Charles' daughter, Annie, dies.

The Great Exhibition is held in London. Many of Britain's new industrial machines and goods are displayed to visitors.

1854

Britain and France join Turkey in the Crimean War against Russia.

1855

In Moravia, Gregor Mendel begins his studies of peas and how features are passed on from generation to generation.

1856

Henry Bessemer invents a way of making large amounts of steel very cheaply.

Darwin starts writing *The Origin of Species*.

1858

18 JUNE: Darwin receives a letter from Alfred Russel Wallace in which Wallace describes his theory of evolution.

30 JUNE: A joint paper on evolution by Wallace and Darwin is presented at the Linnean Society in London.

1859

Darwin's book about natural selection, *The Origin of Species*, is published.

1860

Debate in Oxford between Bishop Sam Wilberforce and Darwin's supporters.

1861

The states of Italy form one country.

The American Civil War begins.

1862

Thomas Huxley publishes *Man's Place in Nature*, in which he argues that humans have ape origins.

1867

The Second Reform Act allows every house-owning man in Britain to vote.

The German philosopher Karl Marx publishes the first volume of *Das Kapital*.

1870

In England, the Education Act says there should be school places for all five-to-twelve-year-olds.

1871

The states of Germany form one country, the German Empire. Darwin's book, *The Descent of Man*, is published.

1872

Darwin's book, *The Expressions of the Emotions in Man and Animals*, is published, the third of his books on evolution.

1876

Charles and Emma become grandparents, but Amy, the wife of their son Francis, dies shortly after giving birth.

1882

APRIL: Charles Darwin dies and is buried in Westminster Abbey.

1884

The Third Reform Act allows more than 2 million men in Britain to vote.

1900

The work of Gregor Mendel is recognized by scientists.

1996

Dolly the sheep becomes the world's first clone of a mammal.

Glossary

Adapted
Suited. Animals and plants are adapted, or suited to their environment.

Ancestor
An earlier type of animal or plant from which others have evolved.

Barnacles
Small sea animals with a hard shell, which stick to rocks and the bottom of ships.

Botanist
A scientist who studies plants.

Clergyman
A person, minister, pastor, rector, priest or rabbi who does religious work.

Democratic
Allowing all the people a say in how a country is ruled.

Domestic
A domestic animal is a type of animal that has been tamed so it can be useful to people. Farm animals are domesticated animals.

Dominant
Most powerful.

Evolution
The process of change over time.

Extinct
Died out; no longer living in the world.

Fossils
Usually the hard parts of plants and animals, such as bones, shells or bark, that have turned to stone and remained in rock.

Genetics
The study of how features are passed on from parents to offspring.

Geologist
A scientist who studies the features of the Earth's crust.

Iguanas
Large lizards.

Inbreeding
Breeding from closely related animals or people.

Indigenous
The first people to live in a place.

Memoirs
A person's writing about their memories of certain events or people.

Missionaries
People who go to spread their religion in other countries.

Naturalist
A scientist who studies animals and plants.

Offspring
Children of animals or people.

Orchids
An orchid is a kind of flower. There are many different types of orchids in tropical countries.

Parish
An area that has its own church.

Postage franks
Marks on a letter to show that someone has paid for postage, like stamps.

Predators
Animals that feed on other animals.

Species
Animals or plants that have been grouped together because they share similar features. Members of a species can breed with each other but not with other species.

Specimens
Animals, plants, rocks or other things that a scientist takes away so that he or she can learn about them.

Zoology
The study of animals.

Further Information

BOOKS FOR YOUNGER READERS

Groundbreakers: Charles Darwin
by Ann Fullick (Heinemann, 2001)

Horrible Science: Evolve or Die
by Phil Gates (Scholastic, 1999)

The Story of Life on Earth
by Nicholas Harris
(Oxford University Press, 1999)

BOOKS FOR OLDER READERS

Charles Darwin: Evolution of a Naturalist
by Richard Milner (Facts on File Inc., 1993)

Darwin
by Adrian Desmond and James Moore
(Penguin, 1991)

Darwin
by Jonathan Howard (Oxford University
Press, 1982)

Darwin: A Life in Science
by John Gribbin and Michael White
(Touchstone, 2000)

WEBSITES

**Charles Darwin Timeline
http://honors.ccsu.ctstateu.edu/Honors/
EText/Darwin/DarwinTimeLine.html**
Timeline of his life, with links to other sites.

**Lycos
www.lycos.com**
Use the search engine to find links to a
biography site, a multimedia article, and other
websites on Darwin.

**Yahoo
http://dir.yahoo.com/Science/Biology/
Evolution/Darwin__Charles_Robert__1809_
1882_/**
Use the search engine to find links to Darwin
and other scientists.

VIDEOS

Charles Darwin – His Life, Journeys and Discoveries
(Cromwell Publications, 1999)

Discovery Channel – Galapagos – Beyond Darwin
(Video Collection Int. Ltd, 1998)

Index

Page numbers in **bold** are pages where there is a photograph or an illustration.